A Note From Rick Renner

I am on a personal quest to see a "revival of the Bible" so people can establish their lives on a firm foundation that will stand strong and endure the test as end-time storm winds begin to intensify.

In order to experience a revival of the Bible in your personal life, it is important to take time each day to read, receive, and apply its truths to your life. James tells us that if we will continue in the perfect law of liberty — refusing to be forgetful hearers, but determined to be doers — we will be blessed in our ways. As you watch or listen to the programs in this series and work through this corresponding study guide, I trust you will search the Scriptures and allow the Holy Spirit to help you hear something new from God's Word that applies specifically to your life. I encourage you to be a doer of the Word He reveals to you. Whatever the cost, I assure you — it will be worth it.

> Thy words were found, and I did eat them;
> and thy word was unto me the joy and rejoicing of mine heart:
> for I am called by thy name, O Lord God of hosts.
> — Jeremiah 15:16

Your brother and friend in Jesus Christ,

Rick Renner

Partnering With the Holy Spirit and Planning for Tomorrow and the Future

Copyright © 2022 by Rick Renner
P.O. Box 702040
Tulsa, OK 74170

Published by Rick Renner Ministries
www.renner.org

ISBN 13: 978-1-68031-994-1

eBook ISBN 13: 978-1-68031-995-8

How To Use This Study Guide

This five-lesson study guide corresponds to *"Partnering With the Holy Spirit and Planning for Tomorrow and the Future" With Rick Renner* (Renner TV). Each lesson in this study guide covers a topic that is addressed during the program series, with questions and references supplied to draw you deeper into your own private study of the Scriptures on this subject.

To derive the most benefit from this study guide, consider the following:

First, watch or listen to the program prior to working through the corresponding lesson in this guide. (Programs can also be viewed at **renner.org** by clicking on the Media/Archives links.)

Second, take the time to look up the scriptures included in each lesson. Prayerfully consider their application to your own life.

Third, use a journal or notebook to make note of your answers to each lesson's Study Questions and Practical Application challenges.

Fourth, invest specific time in prayer and in the Word of God to consult with the Holy Spirit. Write down the scriptures or insights He reveals to you.

Finally, take action! Whatever the Lord tells you to do according to His Word, do it.

For added insights on this subject, it is recommended that you obtain Rick Renner's book *The Holy Spirit and You: Working Together as Heaven's Dynamic Duo*. You may also select from Rick's other available resources by placing your order at **renner.org** or by calling 1-800-742-5593.

TOPIC

Two Reasons Why Prayer Is Not Answered

SCRIPTURES

1. **James 4:1-3** — From whence come wars and fightings among you? come they not hence, even of your lusts that war in your members? Ye lust, and have not: ye kill, and desire to have, and cannot obtain: ye fight and war, yet ye have not, because ye ask not. Ye ask, and receive not, because ye ask amiss, that ye may consume it upon your lusts.

2. **1 Peter 2:11** — Dearly beloved, I beseech you as strangers and pilgrims, abstain from fleshly lusts, which war against the soul.

GREEK WORDS

1. "whence" — **πόθεν** (*pothen*): from where; from whence; from what place

2. "wars" — **πόλεμος** (*polemos*): a full-scale, strategically fought war that is continued with unrelenting force; an intensely fought skirmish

3. "fightings" — **μάχομαι** (*machomai*): to quarrel, dispute, argue, or to get into strife or contention with someone else; to engage in battle; used to picture armed combatants who exchanged blows with deadly weapons; it came to denote men who fought hand to hand, striking, punching, wrangling, and rolling on the ground as they slugged it out with each other; it depicts people who are at odds with each other bickering, squabbling, and slugging it out, not with swords or fists, but with their words

4. "among you" — **ἐν ὑμῖν** (*en humin*): in you; among you; in your midst

5. "even of your lusts" — **ἐκ τῶν ἡδονῶν ὑμῶν** (*ek ton hedonon humon*): the word **ἡδονή** (*hedone*) means obsession with pleasure; a strong negative connotation, and it is where the word hedonism is derived; obsessions

6. "abstain" — **ἀπέχο** (*apecho*): to abstain; to withdraw from; to stay away from; to put distance between oneself and something else; to deliber-

ately or intentionally refrain from something; to put physical distance between oneself and another person, place, or thing

7. "lust" — ἐπιθυμέω (*epithumeo*): from ἐπί (*epi*) and θυμός (*thumos*); ἐπί (*epi*) means over and is an intensifier, and θυμός (*thumos*) is passionate desire; one who is bent over in his craving for something; obsessed; driven; hankering after something

8. "kill" — φονεύω (*phoneuo*): kill; murder; commit homicide; slaughter

9. "desire" — ζῆλος (*zelos*): in a negative sense, a self-consumed person who is driven to get what he wants

10. "to have" — ἐπιτυγχάνω (*epitugchano*): from ἐπί (*epi*) and τυγχάνω (*tugchano*); ἐπί (*epi*) means upon and is an intensifier; τυγχάνω (*tugchano*) means to chance upon, to fall upon, to hit the bullseye, to reach a goal; compounded, to fall upon, to happen upon, to seize, to obtain a goal

11. "cannot obtain" — οὐ δύνασθε (*ou dunasthe*): are unable; are powerless

12. "fight" — μάχομαι (*machomai*): to quarrel, dispute, argue, or to get into strife or contention with someone else; to engage in battle; used to picture armed combatants who exchanged blows using deadly weapons; it came to denote men who fought hand to hand, striking, punching, wrangling, and rolling on the ground as they slugged it out with each other; it depicts people who are at odds with each other bickering, squabbling, and slugging it out, not with swords or fists but with their words

13. "because" — διὰ (*dia*): because; on account of the fact

14. "ask not" — αἰτέω (*aiteo*): αἰτέω (*aiteo*) means to request assistance to meet tangible needs

15. "amiss" — κακῶς (*kakos*): badly; wrongly

16. "consume" — δαπανάω (*dapanao*): waste; to squander one's money, time, energy, resources

17. "upon your lusts" — ἐν ταῖς ἡδοναῖς ὑμῶν (*en tais hedonais humon*): the word ἡδονή (*hedone*) has a strong negative connotation and is where the word hedonism is derived; meaning for your obsessive and hedonistic desires

SYNOPSIS

The five lessons in this study on *Partnering With the Holy Spirit and Planning for Tomorrow and the Future* will focus on the following topics:

- Two Reasons Why Prayer Is Not Answered
- Friendship With the World
- Repentance and the Grace of God
- Evil Speaking
- Planning for Tomorrow and the Future

The emphasis of this lesson:

Out of great pain and loss, the people James was writing to were warring and fighting with each other, using their words as a weapon. Their intense desire for earthly possessions was fueled by selfish motives, which never produced what they hoped for. We must always remember to pray for what we need and make sure our motives are God-focused.

Of all the books of the Bible, the writings of James, the half-brother of Jesus, hold a very unique place in the canon of Scripture. In a very candid, non-condemning way, James tackled hot topics we all face in everyday life. From understanding the source of temptation and the importance of being a *doer* of the Word, to the necessity of taming the tongue and being able to recognize true godly wisdom, the book of James provides relevant truth for every believer in every generation.

The fourth chapter of James is yet another example of this. Here James addresses the root cause of discontentment and irritability and why we often argue and fight with fellow believers. As previously mentioned, he often posed questions to his readers, this time saying:

> **From whence come wars and fightings among you? come they not hence, even of your lusts that war in your members? Ye lust, and have not: ye kill, and desire to have, and cannot obtain: ye fight and war, yet ye have not, because ye ask not. Ye ask, and receive not, because ye ask amiss, that ye may consume it upon your lusts.**
>
> **—James 4:1-3**

To understand the purpose of these verses and grasp the full impact of what's being said, we need to turn our attention back to James' opening words in chapter one for a brief review.

James Wrote His Letter
to Believers Who Were Hurting

James began his letter, saying, "James, a servant of God and of the Lord Jesus Christ, to the twelve tribes which are scattered abroad, greeting" (James 1:1). In this verse, we discover to whom he was writing: Jews from the 12 tribes of Israel who had become believers in Christ and who had also been *scattered abroad.* The words "scattered abroad" are very important. They are a translation of the Greek word *diaspora*, which describes *the random scattering of seed.* Here, this word was used to depict *the scattering of Jewish believers.*

In the First Century world, seed was either planted in a nice, neat row one seed at a time or it was scattered randomly. The word *diaspora* describes this *random scattering.* The sower would reach his hand into a satchel of seed, grab a handful, and then randomly scatter it over a field, throwing a little here and a little there. This is the imagery of what happened to many First Century believers as a result of widespread persecution.

Like seed seized by the hand of the sower, these believers were taken away from family and friends, removed from their homes and jobs, and randomly scattered all over the eastern lands of the Mediterranean without rhyme or reason. They had lost virtually all their personal possessions and finances, and their future looked very bleak. This tells us that the displacement of these believers was not nice, neat, or orderly; it was very disruptive and chaotic.

Knowing who James was writing to — the persecuted believers who were scattered abroad — helps us better understand why he said what he said in the fourth chapter of his letter. These people were really struggling and doing everything they could to regain what they had lost after being evicted from their homeland.

Beginning in James 4:1, let's unpack the deeper meaning of what James was saying.

Out of Great Pain,
People Were at 'War' and 'Fighting'

*From whence come wars and fightings among you? come they
not hence, even of your lusts that war in your members?*
— James 4:1

Immediately, we see in this verse that the believers James was writing to
were fighting among themselves. It seems the reason for the ruckus was,
some of them were being blessed and others were not. Rather than rejoice
with those who were experiencing victory and answers to prayer, those
who were not receiving became angry and bitter. As a result, wars and
fighting were taking place among them.

The word "whence" in Greek is *pothen*, and it means *from where, from
whence*, or *from what place* (were these wars and fightings coming). The
word "wars" is the Greek word *polemos*, which describes *a full-scale, strategically fought war that is continued with unrelenting force.* And the word
"fightings" in Greek is *machomai*, which means *to quarrel, dispute, argue, or
to get into strife or contention with someone else.* It denotes *one who engages
in battle* and is used to picture *armed combatants who exchanged blows using
deadly weapons.*

This word *machomai* ("fightings") came to denote *men who fought hand to
hand, striking, punching, wrangling, and rolling on the ground as they slugged
it out with each other.* Moreover, it depicts people who are at odds with
each other, bickering, squabbling, and slugging it out, not with swords or
fists but **with their words.**

Thus, these "fightings" were a war of words, and James said they were
happening "among you," which in Greek means *in you, among you,* or *in
your midst.* These believers were really slugging it out, hurling insult after
insult against each other in a despicable display of low-level carnality.

Where did these wars and fightings come from? James said, "…Even of
your lusts that war in your members" (James 4:1). In Greek, "even of your
lusts" is *ek ton hedonon humon.* Here the word *hedonon*, a form of the word
hedone, describes *an obsession with pleasure.* It has a strong negative connotation, and it is where we derive the word "hedonism." This is a picture of
someone obsessed with getting what he wants.

Remember, these individuals had lost everything, and when they saw others being blessed, they became obsessed with reclaiming what they'd lost. And this obsession became a "war" inside of them. Again, this word "war" describes *a full-scale war* or *an intensely fought skirmish.*

We Are To 'Abstain From Fleshly Lusts'

This situation James was addressing is reminiscent of what the apostle Peter talked about in his first epistle. He said, "Dearly beloved, I beseech you as strangers and pilgrims, abstain from fleshly lusts, which war against the soul" (1 Peter 2:11).

The Greek word for "beseech" is *parakaleo*, which literally means *to come alongside and call out to someone.* It is the idea of *praying, begging,* or *appealing.* The use of this word is the equivalent of Peter coming to his readers, falling on his knees, and begging them to hear and heed what he is saying.

What was Peter's plea? "…Abstain from fleshly lusts, which war against the soul" (1 Peter 2:11). The word "abstain" is the Greek word *apecho,* which means *to abstain, to withdraw from, to stay away from,* or *to put distance between oneself and something else.* It is *to deliberately or intentionally refrain from something,* and it implies *putting physical distance between oneself and another person, place, or thing.*

Satisfying our fleshly lusts is empty, fleeting, and not worth the energy. We are just strangers and pilgrims passing through this earthly life on to our eternal life in Heaven. When fleshly lusts war against your soul — and they will — you need to put physical distance between yourself and any person, place, or thing that is enticing you to enter into sin. The farther away something is, the harder it is to reach out and grab hold of it.

Intense Desire With Wrong Motives Always Leaves Us Empty

Returning to James' discourse, he said, "Ye lust, and have not: ye kill, and desire to have, and cannot obtain: ye fight and war, yet ye have not, because ye ask not" (James 4:2). The word "lust" here is the Greek word *epithumeo,* which comes from the words *epi* and *thumos.* The word *epi* means *over* and is an intensifier, and *thumos* is *passionate desire.* When these words are compounded to form *epithumeo,* it depicts *one who is bent over in his craving for something.* He is *obsessed, driven,* and *hankering after something.*

In fact, this person is so obsessed, James said, "…Ye kill, and desire to have…" (James 4:2). In Greek, the word "kill" is *phoneuo,* and it means *to kill, murder,* or *commit homicide.* It is intentional murder or slaughter. To be clear, the believers James was writing to were not physically killing each other, but their attitudes and actions toward one another were murderous.

James said they "…desire to have, and cannot obtain…" (James 4:2). The word "desire" is the Greek word *zelos,* which is where we get the word "zeal" or "zealous." In this case, it is portrayed in a negative sense and depicts *a self-consumed person who is driven to get what he wants.* He is so self-focused, he is totally blind to the needs of others. His desire "to have" what he wants is very intense.

The Greek word for "to have" here is *epitugchano,* which is from the words *epi* and *tugchano.* The word *epi* means *upon* and is an intensifier, and the word *tugchano* means *to chance upon, to fall upon, to hit the bullseye,* or *to reach a goal.* When these words are compounded, the new word *epitugchano* means *to fall upon, to happen upon, to seize,* or *to obtain a goal.*

In this case, these believers were unable to seize or happen upon their goal. Specifically, James said they "cannot obtain" it, which in Greek is *ou dunasthe* and means *they are unable or powerless* to hit the bullseye. The reason they are powerless to obtain what they want is, they are going about it the wrong way.

In verse 2, James reiterates the wrong methods these believers were using. He said, "…Ye fight and war, yet ye have not…" (James 4:2). Again, we see that they were "fighting," which is the Greek word *machomai,* meaning *to quarrel, dispute,* or *argue* or *to get into strife or contention with someone else.* However, instead of denoting men who fought hand to hand, striking, punching, and rolling on the ground as they slugged it out with each other, this word *machomai* depicts *people who are at odds with each other, bickering, squabbling, and slugging it out with their words.*

James then added, "…Yet ye have not, because ye ask not" (James 4:2). In Greek, the word "because" is the word *dia,* and here it means *because* or *on account of the fact* that they "asked not." This phrase "ask not" is a translation of the Greek word *aiteo,* which means *to request assistance to meet tangible needs.* This word carries with it a full expectation of receiving an answer. The only problem is, the believers James was writing to in the first part of that verse never prayed! They never went to God and asked Him to get involved and meet their needs.

What Does It Mean To 'Ask Amiss'?

In addition to failing to pray, James noted a second major reason for unanswered pray. He said:

> **Ye ask, and receive not, because ye ask amiss, that ye may consume it upon your lusts.**
>
> — James 4:3

In this verse, the word "amiss" is the Greek word *kakos*, which describes *something done badly or wrongly*. Hence, this could be translated, "You asked but didn't receive because the prayer you prayed was the wrong kind of prayer." The fact is, there are several different kinds of prayer listed in the New Testament. With the help of the Holy Spirit, we need to learn how to pray the right prayer at the right time.

Not only were the believers James was writing to praying the wrong prayers, they also had the wrong motives. Essentially, that is what he meant when he said, "...That ye may consume it upon your lusts" (James 4:3). The word "consume" in Greek is *dapanao*, and it means *to waste* or *to squander one's money, time, energy, or resources*.

The phrase "upon your lusts" in Greek is *en tais hedonais humon*. The word *hedonais* is a form of the word *hedone* and, again, it is where we get the word "hedonism." A more literal translation of this Greek phrase would be, *"You squander your time, energy, and resources for your obsessive and hedonistic desires."* When people like this see God bless someone, they get angry instead of rejoicing with that person. Again, they are totally self-consumed and oblivious to the needs of others or what's best for the Kingdom of God.

Two Things We Must Always Remember To Do

Friend, God wants to bless all His children — including you! His heart's desire is to restore what the enemy has stolen, bringing healing to our bodies, reinstating our finances, and reestablishing our business. The key is to remember that it is in *His timing*. The Bible says, "He hath made every thing beautiful in his time..." (Ecclesiastes 3:11), and our times are in His hand (*see* Psalm 31:15).

In the meantime, God wants us to keep our eyes on Him. He doesn't want us to only think about ourselves. When we're self-absorbed, we can't be Kingdom-minded. Consequently, we begin to sink lower and lower in our thinking until we're slugging it out and angry with other people who have received God's blessings when we haven't. Instead of lusting after things and warring and fighting to get "our share," we need to make sure we've done two things:

First, **we need to pray**. If you haven't asked for God's wisdom and help in what you're about to do or in what you desire to receive, you're off to a wrong start. Prayer paves the way for God to move! He sees all and knows all and, if you'll only ask Him, He will steer you to the right place at the right time to be exceedingly blessed, giving you wisdom and showing you what to do.

Second, **when you do pray, make sure you're Kingdom-minded and open to God's will**. Again, don't be so focused on yourself that you're blind to the needs of others. Know that, like Abraham, God wants to bless you to be a blessing to someone else. It's not all about you. It's all about Him and His desire to save people for eternity, make them His disciples, and see their lives restored and healed. And if someone else has received his answer before you do, rejoice!

STUDY QUESTIONS

Study to shew thyself approved unto God, a workman that needeth not to be ashamed, rightly dividing the word of truth.
— 2 Timothy 2:15

1. Many of us struggle to remember to actually *ask* God for what we need. Why do you think that is? Do we actually have a biblical basis for believing that God hears and will answer our prayers? Read Matthew 7:7,8; John 16:24; 1 John 5:14,15; and Philippians 4:6,7 to find out.

2. It can be a big challenge to trust God to provide for our physical needs. How many times have you found yourself worried about making sure you have enough materially? Read Matthew 6:25-34 and Luke 12:22-32. What promises does Jesus make in these passages that we can stand on as we pray?

PRACTICAL APPLICATION

But be ye doers of the word, and not hearers only,
deceiving your own selves.
— James 1:22

1. What's your normal reaction when you see or hear about others being blessed by God? What usually goes through your mind? Has jealousy been an issue for you personally?

2. James' readers reached a point where they became obsessed with regaining the physical possessions they had lost. Think for a minute: Are there any material things that you're constantly focused on getting? If so, what are they? Pray and ask the Lord to show you why this is such an obsession and how you can overcome the fear that drives it.

3. What tends to keep you from asking God for what you need?

4. Look again at the definition of "abstain" in today's lesson. What's one temptation or desire that you need to distance yourself from? Invite the Holy Spirit to help you avoid the situations, places, people, and things that tend to pull you toward it.

5. What desire(s) do you have that began as normal and healthy, but over time turn into an unhealthy obsession? It might be the desire to be financially stable; to have a godly, fulfilling marriage; to work at a job that is genuinely satisfying and connected to your calling, etc. Ask God for His grace to keep it in the right perspective and to trust Him to meet those needs in His way and timing — His is always better than ours.

LESSON 2

TOPIC

Friendship With the World

SCRIPTURES

1. **James 4:4,5** — Ye adulterers and adulteresses, know ye not that the friendship of the world is enmity with God? whosoever therefore will be a friend of the world is the enemy of God. Do ye think that the scripture saith in vain, The spirit that dwelleth in us lusteth to envy?

GREEK WORDS

1. "adulteresses" — μοιχαλίδες (*moichaledes*): feminine form of μοιχός (*moichos*); one who violates another; to take something illegally; to seduce another person's spouse; one who violates a marital commitment by having a sexual relationship outside the covenant of marriage; adulterer; one who is guilty of indecent sexual behavior

2. "know ye not" — οὐκ οἴδατε (*ouk oidate*): the word οὐκ is emphatic, and οἶδα (*oida*) means to see, perceive, understand, or comprehend

3. "friendship" — φιλία (*philia*): friendship, affection, fondness, love; an intense fondness that is developed between people who enjoy each other's company; two or more people who know one another, who are fond of one another, and who are growing more deeply involved in each other's lives

4. "world" — κόσμος (*kosmos*): the world; depicts anything fashioned or ordered; denotes systems and institutions in society, such as fashion, finances, education, entertainment; world systems

5. "enmity" — ἐχθρός (*echthros*): hatred, hostility; an enemy or opponent; animosity, antagonism, or enmity; describes those who are irreconcilable; depicts enemies in a military conflict; those engaged in a military conflict; hostile enemies

6. "will be" — βούλομαι (*boulomai*): counsel or resolve

7. "friend" — φίλος (*philos*): a beloved friend; dear; friendly; a companion; an associate; held dear in a close bond of affection

8. "is" — καθίστημι (*kathistemi*): to constitute or to render

9. "enemy" — ἐχθρός (*echthros*): hatred, hostility; an enemy or opponent; animosity, antagonism, or enmity; describes those who are irreconcilable; depicts enemies in a military conflict; those engaged in a military conflict; hostile enemies

10. "vain" — κενῶς (*kenos*): in vain; to no purpose; for nothing; without sense; empty; hollow; worthless

11. "dwelleth" — κατοικέω (*katoikeo*): depicts settling down into a new home and making oneself feel comfortable there; a permanent resident

12. "in" — ἐν (*en*): in or inside

13. "lusteth" — ἐπιποθέω (*epipotheo*): an intense desire; a craving, a hunger, an ache, a yearning or hankering for something; a longing or

pining for something; to strain after, to greatly desire; to have strong affection; a fervent passion; an obsession

14. "envy" — φθόνος (*phthonos*): jealousy; a hostile feeling toward someone else because of an advantage, benefit, or position that another has; a deeply felt grudge due to someone possessing what one wishes was his own

SYNOPSIS

In our first lesson, we focused on the importance of doing two specific things to stay connected in partnership with the Holy Spirit. First, we learned the necessity of *praying* before we begin anything. When James wrote to his First-Century audience, they were in a war of words with other believers around them, partly because they hadn't prayed and invited God into what they were doing.

The second cause for the chaos and contention among them was that when they did pray, they were "asking amiss" (James 4:3), or asking God for things with the wrong motives. Specifically, James said they were asking in order to "consume it upon their lusts" (James 4:3). That is, they were *wasting their time, energy, and resources for obsessive and self-indulgent desires.*

Therefore, we must always remember to pray for what we need and make sure our motives are God-focused.

The emphasis of this lesson:

When we give our attention and affection to someone or something other than God, it is the equivalent of spiritual adultery, and it grieves Him deeply. Indeed, friendship with the world makes us a hostile enemy of God. His Spirit who lives in us is envious and jealous of anything or anyone who tries to take His place in our lives.

A Wrong Focus Leads to Wrong Actions

When James wrote his letter, it was written to Jews who had become Christians but were scattered abroad throughout the eastern parts of the Roman Empire. They had lost virtually everything they once had as a result of persecution, and now they were behaving terribly toward one another because they were focused on and obsessed with getting earthly things. James said:

From whence come wars and fightings among you? come they not hence, even of your lusts that war in your members? Ye lust, and have not: ye kill, and desire to have, and cannot obtain: ye fight and war, yet ye have not, because ye ask not. Ye ask, and receive not, because ye ask amiss, that ye may consume it upon your lusts.

— James 4:1-3

(For a detailed review of the original Greek meaning of these verses, please refer back to Lesson 1.)

What Does Spiritual Adultery Look Like?

With the situation among James' readers quickly deteriorating, he seized the authority God had entrusted to him and began to speak correction to their wayward hearts, saying:

Ye adulterers and adulteresses, know ye not that the friendship of the world is enmity with God? whosoever therefore will be a friend of the world is the enemy of God. Do ye think that the scripture saith in vain, The spirit that dwelleth in us lusteth to envy?

— James 4:4,5

Looking back at verse 4, we see that James bluntly called his readers "adulterers and adulteresses." When he addressed them in this manner, it must have felt like a powerful slap in the face to them. More than likely, they had never been spoken to in such harsh tones. Even before they came to Christ, they had been godly, moral Jews who lived according to the Jewish law and would have never committed adultery. So why did James address them in such a way?

What's interesting is that when you look at this opening verse in the Greek text, it doesn't say *adulterers* and *adulteresses*. It simply says "adulteresses," which is the Greek word *moichaledes*, the feminine form of *moichos* ("adulterers"). It describes *one who violates another* or *one who takes something illegally*. It means *to seduce another person's spouse* and denotes *one who violates a marital commitment by having a sexual relationship outside the covenant of marriage*. An adulterer is *one who is guilty of indecent sexual behavior*.

The reason James chose this word *moichaledes* — the word for "adulteresses" — is because he was speaking to the Church, which is also called the Bride of Christ. These particular believers who were a part of the Church had violated their commitment to Christ, the Groom. This was James' way of saying, "You're behaving so badly and have become so obsessed with the world that you are like an unfaithful wife. You've crossed a line, and in the mind of God you have committed spiritual adultery."

These believers were giving their attention, devotion, and affection to someone or something else instead of God, and it was grieving Him deeply.

Friendship With the World
Makes Us God's Enemy

James went on to say, "…Know ye not that the friendship of the world is enmity with God?…" (James 4:4). In Greek, the words "know ye not" are *ouk oidate*. The word *ouk* is very emphatic, and the word *oidate* is a form of the word *oida*, which means *to see, perceive, understand*, or *comprehend*. Thus, the phrase "know ye not" is the equivalent of saying, "Do you all really not understand what you're doing? Have you not comprehended what your actions mean?"

James was appealing to them in the strongest way possible to get their attention. He also used the word "that," which in Greek points to *a very specific conclusion*, and that conclusion is "…friendship of the world is enmity with God" (James 4:4).

The Greek word for "friendship" here is *philia*, and it describes *friendship, affection, fondness*, and *love*. It depicts *an intense fondness that is developed between people who enjoy each other's company*. It indicates *two or more people who know one another, who are fond of one another, and who are growing more deeply involved in each other's lives*.

By using the word *philia* — translated here as "friendship" — James 4:4 tells us that these believers had come to a place where they had grown more and more fond of the world. Day by day they had become more deeply connected with the things of the world, giving increasingly more of their affection and devotion to worldly things — affection and devotion that they were previously giving to God.

We know from our study of James 4:1-3 that these believers were struggling with materialism. Their own lust and desires for various things were causing them to war and fight one another with their words. **The more they fell in love with the world, the more they acted like the world.**

The word "world" in verse 4 is the Greek word *kosmos*, and rather than describe the physical earth, it denotes *world systems and institutions in society*. These include the areas of fashion, finances, education, and entertainment. It depicts anything *fashioned* or *ordered*. Whether intentional or unintentional, it seems James' readers were re-bonding with the "world" (*kosmos*). They were redirecting their time, attention, and affection that was rightfully God's to other things, which in His mind was spiritual adultery.

James said that such friendship with the world is "enmity with God" (James 4:4). This word "enmity" in Greek is *echthros*, and it describes *hatred and hostility, an enemy or opponent, animosity, antagonism*, or *enmity*. It depicts *those who are irreconcilable*, such as *enemies in a military conflict, those engaged in a military conflict*, or *hostile enemies*.

When a believer who has been washed in the Blood and indwelt by the Holy Spirit begins to take the fondness and the affection that belongs to Jesus and redirect it back to the old world he or she was rescued from, it creates an antagonistic situation with God Himself.

How Does a Believer in Love With Jesus Go Back to Loving the World?

The key to understanding how a Christian backslides in his love and devotion to God is found in the second part of James 4:4, which says, "…Whosoever therefore will be a friend of the world is the enemy of God." Notice the two words "will be." In Greek, it is the word *boulomai*, which describes *counsel* or *resolve*. In this case, it literally means *I counsel* or *I advise*. We could even call it *self-talk* or *self-counsel*.

With this in mind, a better translation of this portion of the verse would be, "…Whosoever therefore *counsels and advises himself* to be a friend of the world is the enemy of God." This word *boulomai* — meaning *self-talk* or *self-counsel* — helps us understand the process of how believers drift and begin to shift their fondness and affection off of Jesus and on to other things.

Most Christians who are deeply in love with God don't wake up one day and say, "Today is the day I'm going to backslide. Starting now, I'm going to redirect my love, affection, and fondness for Jesus to the world." On the contrary, when a person who really loves Jesus backslides, it is a very slow, step-by-step departure. Little by little, they counsel and advise themselves (*boulomai*) into making one small exception and compromise at a time.

Consider this example. Two believers who are madly in love with Jesus get invited by friends to go see a new movie that just hit theaters. After reading the reviews, they discover the film is peppered with profanity and also includes a number of sexually explicit scenes. In their gut, they know they shouldn't go, but through self-talk (*boulomai*), they counsel themselves into lowering their standards to go see the movie with their friends.

Well, I know I shouldn't do this, they say to themselves, *but just once won't hurt. Besides, we wouldn't want them to think we're legalistic or judgmental.* Thus, a movie that at one time they would have never attended, they go and see, and their actions place them on a slippery slope to compromise.

Friend, when we compromise doing what's right one time, it's easier to do it the next time and the next time. It is a step-by-step movement in the wrong direction. Sure, we may still be going to church, but something has changed. One little exception at a time, we harden our hearts and lose our spiritual sensitivity to the voice of the Holy Spirit.

This is how we can go from being on fire and in love with Jesus to becoming lukewarm and eventually cold toward Him. Slowly and almost imperceptibly, our thoughts begin to be misdirected. The allurement of the world and all it offers becomes more and more attractive, causing us to think about and even long for all sorts of things more than we think about or long for the Lord. Oftentimes we self-talk ourselves out of God's will and into sin without fully realizing what we've done.

Even Believers Can Counsel Themselves Out of Close Companionship With God

Again, James said, "…Whosoever therefore will be a friend of the world is the enemy of God" (James 4:4). The word "friend" here is again the Greek word *philos*, which describes *a beloved friend.* It depicts *one that is dear or friendly, a companion,* or *an associate.* It is *one who is held dear in a close bond of affection.*

Hence, this verse could read, "Anyone who talks himself into being a companion or treasured friend of the world is the enemy of God." Once more, the word "world" here is the Greek word *kosmos,* describing the *world systems and institutions,* such as fashion, finances, education, or entertainment. Furthermore, the word "is" in Greek is *kathistemi,* meaning *to constitute* or *to render.*

The word "enemy" here is the Greek word *echthros*, which is the same word translated as "enmity" earlier in the verse. Again, it describes *hatred* or *hostility* and depicts *an enemy* or *opponent*. It carries the idea of *animosity, antagonism*, or *enmity* and depicts *hostile enemies who are engaged in a military conflict*.

Keep in mind that James was writing to Christians. Specifically, they were believers who had counseled themselves into becoming dearly loved companions of the world systems. James said that those who did so would make themselves a hostile enemy of God. These believers had crossed a line and put themselves in a wretched place no believer should ever want to be in.

We Have Become the Permanent Home of the Holy Spirit

When we come to verse 5, James spoke rhetorically and asked, "Do ye think that the scripture saith in vain, The spirit that dwelleth in us lusteth to envy?" (James 4:5) The word "vain" here is the Greek word *kenos*, which means *in vain, to no purpose*, or *for nothing*. Something "vain" is something *without sense, empty, hollow*, or *worthless*. In this verse, James was asking his readers, "Do you think that the Scriptures say *to no purpose* or *for no reason* that the Spirit that dwelleth in us lusteth to envy?"

In Greek, the word "dwelleth" is very important. It is the word *katoikeo*, which is a compound of the word *kata*, meaning *down*, and the word *oikeo*, which is the word for *a house*. When these words are compounded, it pictures *one settling down into a new home and making himself feel comfortable there*. It denotes *a permanent resident*.

Who has taken up permanent residency? Who has made Himself comfortable and has settled down into a new home? The Bible says it is the Holy Spirit. Where is He dwelling? Scripture says "in us" (James 4:5). The word "in" is the Greek word *en*, and it means *in* or *inside*. Hence, the Holy Spirit's presence is living *inside* us. This means everywhere we go and in everything we do, we carry the Holy Spirit with us.

So if we begin to give our attention and affection to the things of this world instead of giving them to God, the Holy Spirit becomes deeply grieved. He feels the pain of one who is betrayed, which is why He calls this an act of spiritual adultery. Again, James said, "…The spirit that dwelleth in us lusteth to envy" (James 4:5).

The Holy Spirit Is Jealous for Our Love

This strange word "lusteth" is the Greek word *epipotheo*, which is a compound of the word *epi*, meaning *over*, and the word *potheo*, meaning *to yearn* or *to hanker after something*. When these words are joined together, it describes *an intense desire* or *a craving, a hunger, an ache, a yearning, or a hankering for something*. It is *a longing or pining for something*. Moreover, it means *to strain after, to greatly desire*; or *to have strong affection*. Who is the one with such a fervent passion and an obsession? It is the Holy Spirit living in you, and He is craving and hungering and longing after *you*!

When the Scripture says the Spirit "lusteth to envy," the Greek word for "envy" is *phthonos*, which is essentially *jealousy*. It depicts *a hostile feeling toward someone else because of an advantage, benefit, or position that another has*. This word *phthonos* also describes *a deeply felt grudge due to someone possessing what one wishes was his own*. We could say this word is a picture of a jilted lover who is irate that the love and affection he was once receiving is now being given to another.

Friend, the jilted lover here is none other than the Holy Spirit. Filled with envy and jealousy, He doesn't sit idly by and pout or have a pity party. Rather, He puts into motion a rescue operation to get back the person who is rightfully His. And He is willing to do whatever is necessary to succeed in His quest. Thus, the Holy Spirit that dwells in us yearns and craves (*epipotheo*) to have us all to Himself; He doesn't want to share us with anyone else.

Taking into account the original Greek meaning of all these words, here is the *Renner Interpretive Version* (*RIV*) of James 4:5:

> **The Spirit, who has come to settle down, to permanently dwell, and to make His home in us, has an all-consuming, ever-growing, passionate desire to possess us — and He is envious and filled with malice toward anything or anyone who tries to take His place in our lives.**

Friend, are you passionately in love with Jesus? Does He still hold first place in your life? Are you still giving Him your complete love and devotion? Have you become distracted and enticed by the things of this world? Or are you somewhere in the middle? If you're giving your *best* attention and affection to someone or something other than God, His Spirit in you is grieving. Know that it's never too late to run back into Jesus' arms — He's waiting!

STUDY QUESTIONS

Study to shew thyself approved unto God, a workman that
needeth not to be ashamed, rightly dividing the word of truth.
— 2 Timothy 2:15

1. What do First Corinthians 3:16 and 6:19; Second Corinthians 6:16; and Ephesians 2:22 say about your relationship with the Holy Spirit?
2. Have you ever had a callus form on your hand or foot? If so, you have experienced a real-life example of what sometimes happens to believers' hearts. What does Paul have to say in Acts 28:26,27; First Timothy 4:1,2; and Second Timothy 4:3,4 about the danger of having a callused heart?
3. Just like James, the apostles John and Paul, as well as Jesus Himself, also warned us about friendship with the world. What stands out to you from their words in these passages?
   - 1 John 2:15-17
   - Romans 12:1,2; Colossians 3:1-10
   - Luke 21:34-36

PRACTICAL APPLICATION

But be ye doers of the word, and not hearers only,
deceiving your own selves.
— James 1:22

1. James' readers were behaving so badly and had become so obsessed with chasing after the things of the world that they were acting like unfaithful wives. Knowing that, is there an area of your life where you think you've crossed a spiritual line or been unfaithful to God? Where do you find yourself quietly ignoring the conviction of the Holy Spirit?
2. In your own words, explain how a person can go from being on fire and in love with Jesus to becoming lukewarm and eventually cold

toward Him. Have you ever experienced this kind of regression in your walk with God? What things in this world tend to have an alluring effect on you, pulling your attention and affection away from Him?

3. Who do you know who was once on fire for God that has drastically backed away from or is even no longer a believer? What did you see happen in their life that caused them to begin to pull away from Jesus or compromise what they knew to be right? Are there any warning signs you can recognize and watch for in your own life?

LESSON 3

TOPIC

Repentance and the Grace of God

SCRIPTURES

1. **James 4:5-10** — Do ye think that the scripture saith in vain, The spirit that dwelleth in us lusteth to envy? But he giveth more grace. Wherefore he saith, God resisteth the proud, but giveth grace unto the humble. Submit yourselves therefore to God. Resist the devil, and he will flee from you. Draw nigh to God, and he will draw·nigh to you. Cleanse your hands, ye sinners; and purify your hearts, ye double minded. Be afflicted, and mourn, and weep: let your laughter be turned to mourning, and your joy to heaviness. Humble yourselves in the sight of the Lord, and he shall lift you up.

GREEK WORDS

1. "vain" — κενῶς (*kenos*): in vain; to no purpose; for nothing; without sense

2. "dwelleth" — κατοικέω (*katoikeo*): depicts settling down into a new home and making oneself to feel comfortable there; a permanent resident

3. "in" — ἐν (*en*): in or inside

4. "lusteth" — ἐπιποθέω (*epipotheo*): an intense desire; a craving, a hunger, an ache, a yearning or hankering for something; a longing or

pining for something; to strain after, to greatly desire; to have strong affection; a fervent passion; an obsession

5. "envy" — φθόνος (*phthonos*): jealousy; a hostile feeling toward someone else because of an advantage, benefit, or position that another has; a deeply felt grudge due to someone possessing what one wishes was his own

6. "but" — δὲ (*de*): however; emphatically; categorically

7. "resisteth" — ἀντιτάσσομαι (*antitassomai*): to arrange oneself against; to methodically oppose; a strategic plan of opposition intended to bring a situation under control

8. "proud" — ὑπερήφανος (*huperephanos*): from ὑπερ (*huper*) and φανος (*phanos*); ὑπερ (*huper*) depicts something that is above or superior, and φανος (*phanos*) means to be manifested; when compounded, it paints a picture of a person who sees himself above the rest of the crowd; one who is arrogant, haughty, high-and-mighty, impudent; an insolent attitude

9. "humble" — ταπεινός (*tapeinos*): one who has become humble; to reduce one's self-importance; to make small; to minimize oneself; to be willing to stoop to any measure that is needed

10. "submit" — ὑποτάσσω (*hupotasso*): submission; to get things in order; obedience to authority; describes submission to authority in any context; to hide behind someone's back, showing that there is protection in submission

11. "resist" — ἀνθίστημι (*anthistemi*): to stand against; to stand in opposition; it demonstrates the attitude of one who is fiercely opposed to something and therefore determines to do everything within his power to resist it; to stand against it; to withstand; to defy

12. "flee" — φεύγω (*pheugo*): to flee, to take flight, to run away, to run as fast as possible, or to escape; the picture of one's feet flying as he runs from a situation; it was used to depict a lawbreaker who flees in terror from a city or a nation where he broke the law; on rarer occasions it could mean to be charged with a crime, or to be exiled

13. "sinners" — ἁμαρτωλοί (*hamartoloi*): plural, those who keep missing the mark; those who keep falling short of what God expects and approves

14. "purify" — ἁγνίζω (*hagnidzo*): from ἁγνός (*hagnos*), purified and free from defilement; pure inside and out; the word ἁγνίζω (*hagnidzo*) represents the process of doing whatever is necessary to be free from

defilement and to be cleansed; though the water is the agent that cleanses, the worshiper must extend his hands into the ceremonial water to receive cleaning; hence, participation involved

15. "hearts"— **καρδία** (*kardia*): plural, hearts; the core of one's being; hence, the deepest level possible; a deep cleansing

16. "double minded"— **δίψυχος** (*dipsuchos*): plural, those who have two souls; two minds; as a result of being double-minded, this one is pulled in two directions, constantly fluctuating in what he believes, says, or does; one who is unstable, undecided, wavering, wishy-washy

17. "joy"— **χαρά** (*chara*): lightheartedness

18. "heaviness"— **κατήφεια** (*katepheia*): a looking downward in contemplation

19. "humble yourselves"— **ταπεινός** (*tapeinos*): one who has become humble; to reduce one's self-importance; to make small; to minimize oneself; to be willing to stoop to any measure that is needed

20. "lift you up"— **ὑψόω** (*hupsoo*): referring to the highest or most eminent place; pictures a place of dignity; thus, to elevate or exalt one to a place of eminence and dignity

SYNOPSIS

At this point you may be thinking, *What in the world does all this stuff about friendship with the world and being an enemy of God have to do with partnering with the Holy Spirit?* That's a good question.

If you maintain a healthy relationship with the Lord and His Spirit, you will experience a rich, ever-growing partnership with Him where He'll heal your past hurts, lead you in your present moment and help you plan for your tomorrow. However, if you begin to take your eyes off of Jesus and let yourself be attracted to the world's empty distractions, you'll grieve the Holy Spirit and jeopardize your partnership with Him.

Make no mistake: our God is a jealous God, and His Spirit who lives in you wants you all to Himself! He craves and longs for your time, your attention, and your affection. Creating an environment where He feels honored and welcomed is one of the best things you can do to stay close to Him.

The emphasis of this lesson:

God loves us so much that He doesn't wait for us to return to Him. Instead, He causes His grace to swing into action and do for us what we're not doing for ourselves. He resists us to wake us up to our true condition so we'll repent and come back to Him. The moment we realize we've strayed from our devotion to Him and begin to sincerely repent, He stops resisting us, and His blessings begin to flow again.

Unfaithfulness to God Is Like Spiritual Adultery

In James 4:1-3, James candidly questioned his readers as to why they had been arguing and fighting among themselves in a war of words. It seems their relational interaction had deteriorated into a low-level, verbal free-for-all. As a result of harsh persecution and forced dispersion, they had lost virtually everything. Now a number of them were verbally slugging it out, trying desperately to reestablish their lives and regain what they had lost.

Out of genuine concern, James shined a searchlight of truth on the root cause of their backbiting and bickering: an ungodly obsession with material gain and earthly pleasures had become the dominant, driving force of their lives. Instead of praying and asking God for help, many didn't pray at all — or if they did pray, they prayed with the wrong motives.

With all the bluntness we've come to know from James, he turned to his readers and said, "Ye adulterers and adulteresses, know ye not that the friendship of the world is enmity with God?..." (James 4:4). This was James's way of saying, "You are behaving so badly and have become so obsessed with the world that you're like an unfaithful spouse. You've crossed a line, and in God's mind you've committed spiritual adultery."

Be Careful Not To Counsel Yourself Into Sin

How did this happen? James tells us in the second part of verse 4: "...Whosoever therefore will be a friend of the world is the enemy of God" (James 4:4). The phrase "will be" in Greek is the word *boulomai*, which literally means *I counsel* or *I advise*. It is a picture of a person talking to himself and counseling himself to compromise his godly standards and embrace the world's way of thinking. Slowly but surely, one little exception at a time, he advises himself (*boulomai*), and his red-hot love for the Lord grows cold. At the same time, he begins to give his best attention and affection to something or someone else.

Sadly, this person used to enjoy the Bible regularly, pray in the Spirit with sincerity, and speak faith-filled words over his life and the lives of others. Now he doesn't read Scripture, he rarely ever prays, and his joy for the things of God is a mere shadow of what it used to be. Surprisingly, he thinks everything is okay because he's still going to church and giving his tithe, but in reality he's crossed a line into spiritual adultery and has rendered himself a hostile enemy of God.

The Holy Spirit Lives Inside You

At this point, James said, "Do ye think that the scripture saith in vain, The spirit that dwelleth in us lusteth to envy?" (James 4:5) The Greek word for "vain" here is *kenos*, which means *in vain; to no purpose*; or *for nothing*. Hence, James is asking his readers, "Do you think that the Scripture says *for no purpose* or *to no avail* that the Spirit that dwelleth in us lusteth to envy?"

The word "dwelleth" here is the Greek word *katoikeo*, which is a compound of the word *kata*, meaning *down*, and a form of the word *oikos*, the word for *a house*. When compounded, these words form *katoikeo*, which pictures *one who settles down into a new home and makes it his permanent residency*. The Bible says the Holy Spirit has made Himself comfortable and settled down "in us" (James 4:5). This word "in" is the Greek word *en*, and it means *in* or *inside*, which pinpoints the location of the Holy Spirit's presence — *inside us*.

Regrettably, the Holy Spirit is largely ignored by many believers He lives in, which is to their detriment. Friend, if you're a believer, the fullness of God lives inside of you in the Person of the Holy Spirit. That means all God is — all His power, all His wisdom, all His authority — is in you! Therefore, it's in your best interest to learn how to partner with and not ignore or grieve Him.

The Holy Spirit Hungers for You

Again, James says, "…The spirit that dwelleth in us lusteth to envy" (James 4:5). This word "lusteth" in Greek is the word *epipotheo*, which is a compound of the words *epi* and *potheo*. The word *epi* means *over* and serves as an intensifier, and the word *potheo* means *to yearn for, to long for*, or *to hanker after something*. When these words are compounded, it describes *an intense desire, a craving,* or *a hunger for something.* In context here, it pictures the *fervent passion, craving,* and *hunger* the Holy Spirit has for you!

The Holy Spirit wants to fill you and possess you! He is literally pining for your attention and affection. Each day is a new opportunity for Him to connect with you more closely and fill you with His presence. He wants all of you to Himself, which is what the Scripture means when it says, "...[He] lusteth to envy" (James 4:5). The word "envy" here is the Greek word *phthonos,* which denotes *jealousy.* It is *a hostile feeling toward someone else because of an advantage, benefit, or position that another has.* It can even describe *a deeply felt grudge due to someone possessing what one wishes was his own.*

What James is telling us in this verse is that when we give our affection and devotion to something or someone other than the Lord (who deserves it), His Spirit in us burns with envy. What's more, this word *phthonos* — translated here as "envy" — also carries with it the idea of a scorned lover who is driven to take action. Instead of sitting idly by, he puts a plan in motion to win back the love of his life. In this case, the jilted lover is the Holy Spirit, and He will move Heaven and earth to set you free from whatever has stolen your attention away from Him. He dwells in you and intensely desires (*epipotheo*) to be welcomed in your life.

God 'Resisteth the Proud'

Adding to this, James tells us how God intends to carry out His rescue mission. He says, "But he giveth more grace. Wherefore he saith, God resisteth the proud, but giveth grace unto the humble" (James 4:6).

The opening word "but" is the Greek word *de,* which is like an exclamation point announcing what he is about to say. It is the equivalent of him saying, "*However...,*" "*Emphatically...,*" or "*Categorically,* He gives more grace...." This portion of verse 6 indicates if we won't return to the Holy Spirit on our own, He will swing into action and do whatever it takes to get us to redirect our attention and affection back to Him. His actions are a work of grace.

James goes on to say, "...Wherefore he saith, God resisteth the proud..." (James 4:6). The word "resisteth" here is the Greek word *antitassomai,* which is a combination of the words *anti* and *tassomai.* The word *anti* means *against,* and the word *tassomai* means *to order or arrange.* When these words are compounded to form *antitassomai,* it means *to arrange oneself against* or *to methodically oppose*. It depicts *a strategic plan of opposition intended to bring a situation under control*. Thus, this could be translated, "…God, therefore, arranges Himself against the proud…" or "…God, therefore, methodically opposes the proud and sets into motion a strategic plan of opposition intended to bring the situation back under control…."

The Proud Are the Unrepentant

Who is God resisting and opposing? The Bible says those who are "proud," which is the Greek word *huperephanos*, from the words *huper* and *phanos*. The word *huper* depicts *something that is above or superior*, and *phanos* means *to be manifested*. When these words are compounded, it paints a picture of *a person who sees himself above the rest of the crowd*. It is *one who is arrogant, haughty, high-and-mighty, impudent, and has an insolent attitude*.

Essentially, in this passage, the person who is "proud" (*huperephanos*) is one who is *unrepentant*. He hears the message, feels the conviction of the Holy Spirit, and knows he's drifted in his devotion to God. He needs to come back to Him, but rather than realize how serious his spiritual condition is, he becomes impudent, insolent, and stubborn and won't budge.

Thankfully, God loves us so much that He doesn't wait for us to return to Him. Instead, He causes His grace to swing into action and do for us what we're not doing for ourselves. This involves, believe it or not, Him resisting any believer who is acting "proud." He sets in motion a strategic plan to oppose and stop them. Why? It's not because He's *against* them, but because He's *for* them. He's trying to get them to wake up to their condition so they'll repent and come back to Him.

Friend, when God puts His hand out to stop you, you're stopped. He will bring everything in your life to a screeching halt if necessary, in order to get your attention and affection back on Him! If you're feeling resistance in your life, before you stop to deal with the devil, first pray and ask God, "Am I doing anything that is causing You to resist me or put my life on pause? If so, what is it?"

Humbling Yourself and Submitting to God Empowers You To Resist the Devil

The good news is that the moment you wake up and realize you've strayed from your devotion to God, if you'll turn to Him and ask Him to forgive you, He will. Simply ask: "Lord, I have veered away from You. I've given my attention, fondness, and devotion to something else. Please forgive me and help me put my eyes back on You. In Jesus' name. Amen."

James calls this an act of *grace*. The moment you wake up and begin to sincerely repent, grace swings into action. God stops resisting you and His blessings begin to flow again. The Bible says, "…[God] giveth grace unto the humble" (James 4:6). The word "humble" here is a form of the Greek word *tapeinos*, and it describes *one who has become humble* or *one willing to stoop to any measure that is needed to reduce one's self-importance*. It also means *to make small* or *to minimize oneself*.

The act of humbling oneself is closely connected with James' instruction in verse 7, which says, "Submit yourselves therefore to God. Resist the devil, and he will flee from you" (James 4:7). In Greek, the word "submit" is *hupotasso*, which means *to get things in order*. It also signifies *obedience to God's authority* and describes *submission to authority* in any context. What's interesting is that this word *hupotasso* is also a picture of *a person hiding behind someone's back*, which tells us that there is protection in submission.

Only in a position of submission can you successfully "resist" the devil. This word "resist" in Greek is *anthistemi*, which means *to stand against* or *to stand in opposition*. It demonstrates *the attitude of one who is fiercely opposed to something and therefore determines to do everything within his power to resist it*. It means *to stand against it; to withstand;* or *to defy*.

The Bible says when you resist the devil, "…He will flee from you" (James 4:7). The word "flee" is the Greek word *pheugo*, and it means *to flee, to take flight, to run away, to run as fast as possible*, or *to escape*. It is the picture of one's feet flying as he runs from a situation. This word was used to depict a lawbreaker who flees in terror from a city or a nation where he broke the law, and on rarer occasions, it could mean to be charged with a crime, or to be exiled.

What James is telling us in this verse is that when you submit to God, realigning yourself under His authority, you are empowered to successfully resist the devil and anything he brings against you. And in that position of submission, the devil will "flee" from you — just like a criminal who flees in terror after breaking the law. Indeed, the devil is terrified of a person who is living in right relationship with God.

Draw Near to God…
Cleanse Your Hands and Purify Your Hearts

When we come to James 4:8, it says, "Draw nigh to God, and he will draw nigh to you. Cleanse your hands, ye sinners; and purify your hearts, ye double minded." In Greek, the words "draw near" mean *to get as near as possible*. Like a magnet attracts metal, when you humble yourself and get as close to God as you can, His presence will be strongly attracted into your life.

Notice that James called his readers "sinners," using the plural form of the Greek word *hamartoloi*. This word describes *those who keep missing the mark* or *those who keep falling short of what God expects and approves*. He's not using this term to judge or condemn them, but saying, "Hey, you're missing the bullseye of what God expects, so *purify* your hearts."

The word "purify" here is the Greek word *hagnidzo*, which is from the word *hagnos*, indicating *something purified and free from defilement* or *something pure inside and out*. The word *hagnidzo* represents *the process of doing whatever is necessary to be free from defilement and to be cleansed*. For example, though water is the agent that cleanses, the person must extend and put their hands into the water to be cleansed. Without participation, no cleansing takes place.

What needs to be purified? The Bible says our "hearts." In Greek, this is the plural form of the word *kardia*, and it describes *the core of one's being*. Hence, the deepest level possible. James was instructing his readers — including *us* — to pursue the deepest cleansing we can. He then wrapped up the verse by calling his listeners "double minded," which is the Greek word *dipsuchos*, and it literally means *those who have two souls or two minds*.

A person who is "double-minded" is *one pulled in two directions, constantly fluctuating in what he believes, says, or does*. It is a picture of *one who is unstable, undecided, wavering*, or *wishy-washy*. A double-minded person wants to serve the Lord one day, and the next day he is preoccupied with the things of the world. The only way to break free and stay free from being double minded is to actively participate in the cleansing process by applying the blood of Jesus to our hearts and washing in the water of God's Word.

If You Humble Yourself
God Will Elevate You to a Place of Dignity

James continued, "Be afflicted, and mourn, and weep: let your laughter be turned to mourning, and your joy to heaviness" (James 4:9). The word "joy" — the Greek word *chara* — refers to *lightheartedness*, and the word "heaviness" in Greek is *katepheia*, which describes *a looking downward in contemplation*. Rather than flippantly acting as though everything is fine, James challenged his readers to take time to really think about changing their actions.

Then in the very next verse, we arrive at the main objective of what God has been after all along. It says, **"Humble yourselves in the sight of the Lord, and he shall lift you up"** (James 4:10). Clearly, God's desire is to *lift us up* and *restore* us in every area of our lives. But before He can do that, He needs us to "humble ourselves."

This phrase "humble yourselves" is again a form of the Greek word *tapeinos*, which describes *one who has become humble*. It means *to reduce one's self-importance*; *to make small*; or *to minimize oneself*. It depicts *one willing to stoop to any measure that is needed in order to get things right with God*.

Remember, God wants to "lift you up." This is a translation of the Greek word *hupsoo* and refers to *the highest or most eminent place*. It pictures *a place of dignity*. Thus, it means *to elevate or exalt one to a place of eminence and dignity*. That is what God deeply desires to do in your life.

Friend, if you've strayed away from God, He is calling you to come back home to Him right now. Your journey back begins with recognizing and admitting your spiritual condition and asking Him to forgive you for pursuing other things at the expense of pursuing Him. This demonstrates a humble, contrite heart. Remember, if you humble yourself and draw near to God, He will draw near to you. If you're willing to do whatever He asks you to do, your submission will start the process for God to bring you from a low place back to an extremely high place of dignity, which is what He wants to do for you.

STUDY QUESTIONS

Study to shew thyself approved unto God, a workman that
needeth not to be ashamed, rightly dividing the word of truth.
— 2 Timothy 2:15

1. According to the original Greek, one who is "proud" is *arrogant, haughty, high-and-mighty, impudent, and sees himself above the rest of the crowd.* Be honest with yourself: Can you see this attitude manifesting in any area of your life? If so, where?

2. What does God say about the deadliness of pride in these passages?
   - Psalm 10:4
   - Proverbs 11:2; 16:18
   - Proverbs 16:5; 29:23
   - Proverbs 13:10; 21:4
   - Proverbs 26:12; Isaiah 5:21 (Proverbs 3:3-7; Romans 12:16)

3. The only cure for pride is *humility.* Check out these verses and discover some of the blessings this priceless virtue brings into your life.
   - Matthew 23:12; Luke 14:11; Psalm 147:6
   - Proverbs 3:34; James 4:6; 1 Peter 5:5
   - Psalm 25:9
   - Micah 6:8; Matthew 18:4
   - Isaiah 57:15
   - Proverbs 22:4

PRACTICAL APPLICATION

But be ye doers of the word, and not hearers only,
deceiving your own selves.
— James 1:22

1. So many of us don't relate to God as a fiercely jealous lover, which is why we're so easily wooed and distracted by the world. How do you see God: as your parole officer constantly watching for you to mess up, or do you see Him as the loving, caring husband He wants to be for you?

2. Are you feeling resistance in your life? Does it seem as though you've hit a brick wall, or that you're surrounded and unable to move forward? Before you automatically assume it's the devil, take a moment to pray and ask God, "Am I doing anything that's causing You to resist me? Are You the One pressing 'pause' on my life? If so, why? What are You bringing to the surface that I need to deal with?"

3. When we draw near to God, He promises to draw near to us (*see* James 4:8). Can you remember the last time you felt close to Jesus? What was the atmosphere like in those moments? Do you remember saying or doing anything specific that really opened the door for Him to move in your life?

LESSON 4

TOPIC
Evil Speaking

SCRIPTURES

1. **James 4:11,12** — Speak not evil one of another, brethren. He that speaketh evil of his brother, and judgeth his brother, speaketh evil of the law, and judgeth the law: but if thou judge the law, thou art not a doer of the law, but a judge. There is one lawgiver, who is able to save and to destroy: who art thou that judgest another?

GREEK WORDS

1. "speak not evil" — **μὴ καταλαλεῖτε** (*me katalaleite*): **μὴ** is a negative, thus a prohibition; **καταλαλέω** (*katalaleo*) is a compound of **κατά** (*kata*) meaning down, and **λαλέω** (*laleo*) means to talk or to converse; compounded, to talk down; to denigrate; to speak down about someone else; to verbally defame a person

2. "one of another" — **ἀλλήλων** (*allelon*): each other; reciprocally; of each other

3. "brethren" — **ἀδελφός** (*adelphos*): plural; a term used to describe two or more who were born from the same womb; an endearing term used to describe those of one's own family; later used in a military sense to depict brothers in battle; a comrade; hence, brotherhood

4. "speaketh evil" — **καταλαλέω** (*katalaleo*): a compound of **κατά** (*kata*) meaning down, and **λαλέω** (*laleo*) means to talk or to converse; compounded, to talk down; to denigrate; to speak down about someone else; to verbally defame a person

5. "judgeth" — **κρίνω** (*krino*): a word that usually referred to a jury who had just handed down their final sentence in a court of law; a verdict or a final sentence pronounced as the result of a court trial; after all the evidence had been presented and the judge had examined all the facts, a final verdict was issued by the court; judged legally or by the court of public opinion

6. "law" — **νόμος** (*nomos*): the law of liberty referred to in James 1:25

7. "but if" — **εἰ δὲ** (*ei de*): if, however

8. "judge" — **κρίνω** (*krino*): a word that usually referred to a jury who had just handed down their final sentence in a court of law; a verdict or a final sentence pronounced as the result of a court trial; after all the evidence had been presented and the judge had examined all the facts, a final verdict was issued by the court; judged legally or by the court of public opinion

9. "not a doer of the law" — **οὐκ εἰ ποιητὴς νόμου** (*ouk ei poietes nomou*): **ouk** is emphatic; **ποιητὴς** (*poitetes*) is a creative doer; hence, not one who carries out the performance of the law

10. "one lawgiver" — **ὁ νομοθέτης** (*ho vomothetes*): the one who set the law in place; a law-giver

11. "able" — **δυνάμενος** (*dunamenos*): literally, being able; from **δύναμαι** (*dunamai*), one with power and ability; from **δύναμις** (*dunamis*), which is explosive, superhuman power that comes with enormous energy and produces phenomenal, extraordinary, and unparalleled results; the word used by the Roman army to denote the full strength of troops marching forward to take new territory; used to depict a force of nature, like an earthquake, hurricane, or tornado

12. "save" — **σῴζω** (*sodzo*): to heal, but conveys the idea of wholeness or salvation; wholeness in every part of life; a touch of salvation that brings delivering and healing power that results in wholeness; to deliver one's country from enemies; to protect, keep safe, to keep under protection

13. "destroy" — **ἀπόλλυμι** (*apollumi*): to undo; to destroy; to perish

14. "who art thou" — **σὺ δὲ τίς εἶ** (*su de tis ei*): who; whoever you are

15. "another" — τὸν πλησίον (*ton plesion*): with a definite article, the one near you; the one living in your neighborhood; the nearby neighbor

SYNOPSIS

The First-Century believers James was writing to had certainly been through a great deal. As a result of widespread persecution, they had been ejected from their homes and had lost virtually all of their possessions. Time had passed, and it appears that as some began to be blessed and others were not, those who were without began to verbally assault and slug it out with others. In fact, their waning devotion to God and renewed affection for the things of the world prompted James to call them *adulterers* and *adulteresses*. They had crossed a spiritual line and were behaving like unfaithful spouses. Their atrocious behavior was deeply grieving the Holy Spirit.

The apostle Paul issued a sober warning to us in Ephesians 4:30 saying, "And grieve not the holy Spirit of God…." When we grieve the Holy Spirit, it affects our partnership with Him and disrupts the flow of His presence and power in our lives. Instead of grieving the Spirit, we want to do our best to create an environment where He feels welcome and at home. This is what James was urging his readers to do.

The emphasis of this lesson:

James urged believers not to speak evil of one another — to stop verbally denigrating and defaming each other. Since the flesh always gravitates toward judgment, we must guard our hearts and minds from giving place to this tendency. Whatever we give to others is what we eventually will receive. God and God alone is the judge and lawgiver who has the power to save and destroy.

The Holy Spirit's Work in You Is Permanent, Passionate, and Personal

To jolt and jar his listeners out of the fleshly, self-focused fit, James asked them, "Do ye think that the scripture saith in vain, The spirit that dwelleth in us lusteth to envy?" (James 4:5) We've seen that the word "dwelleth" is the Greek word *katoikeo*, which is a compound of the word *kata*, meaning *down*, and a form of the word *oikos*, which is the term for *a house*. When these words are compounded to form *katoikeo*, it pictures *one who settles down into a new home and makes it his permanent residency.*

This verse is a picture of the Holy Spirit moving into a believer's life, laying his own rugs on the floor, hanging his own pictures on the wall, and placing his favorite chair in the living room. This word "dwelleth" tells us He is not a guest; He is a permanent resident, which means our heart is not a hotel — it is a house. And the Holy Spirit has made Himself comfortable and has settled down "in us" (James 4:5). The word "in" is the Greek word *en*, and it means *in* or *inside*, which pinpoints the place of the Holy Spirit's presence — *inside us.*

James said, "…The spirit that dwelleth in us lusteth to envy" (James 4:5). The Greek word for "lusteth" here is *epipotheo*, which is a compound of the words *epi* and *potheo*. The word *epi* means *over* and is used as an intensifier; and the word *potheo* means *to yearn for, to long for,* or *to hanker after something.* When compounded to form the word *epipotheo*, it describes *an intense desire* or *a craving* for something. It is *the picture of a person doubled over in fervent passion, hungering for something.*

In this case, it is the Holy Spirit bent over pining for *you*! He wants to fill you with His extraordinary power and presence in exchange for your total devotion to Him. With each passing day, He will reveal something new in you that He wants you to surrender to Him. He desires all of you to Himself, which is why the Bible says, "…[He] lusteth to envy" (James 4:5).

The word "envy" here is the Greek word *phthonos*, which is *a hostile feeling toward someone else because of an advantage, benefit, or position that another has.* This word depicts the emotions of a man or woman who has just discovered that their spouse has committed adultery. Rather than do nothing or surrender in defeat, this word *phthonos* — translated here as "envy" — carries with it the idea of one who puts a plan in motion to win back the love of his life.

What James is telling us in this verse is that the jilted lover is the Holy Spirit, and He will move Heaven and earth to set you free from anything that has taken your attention away from Him. He dwells in you and intensely yearns (*epipotheo*) to have you all to Himself. If you have given your affection and devotion to something or someone else instead of Him, He will launch a rescue mission to bring you back home.

The Holy Spirit Always Seeks
To Restore Relationship With Us

How does God intend to make you His own once again? James said, "But he giveth more grace. Wherefore he saith, God resisteth the proud, but giveth grace unto the humble" (James 4:6). For any believer who will not return to the Holy Spirit on their own, God will swing into action and do whatever it takes to regain their love and affection. His actions are a work of grace.

Notice James said, "…God resisteth the proud…" (James 4:6). In Greek, the word "resisteth" is the word *antitassomai*, which is a combination of the words *anti* and *tassomai*. The word *anti* means *against*, and the word *tassomai* means *to order or arrange*. When these words are combined to form *antitassomai*, it means *to arrange oneself against* or *to methodically oppose*.

That's what God does to the proud. He launches *a strategic plan of opposition intended to bring the situation under control*. Thus, this part of the verse could be translated, "…God, therefore, arranges Himself against the proud…" or "…God, therefore, methodically opposes the proud and sets into motion a strategic plan of opposition intended to bring the situation back under control…."

Who is God resisting and opposing? James says those who are "proud." In Greek, this is the word *huperephanos*, which is from the words *huper* and *phanos*. The word *huper* depicts *something that is above or superior*, and *phanos* means *to be manifested*. When these words are compounded, it paints a picture of *a person who sees himself above the rest of the crowd; one who is arrogant, haughty, high-and-mighty, impudent, and has an insolent attitude.*

A person who is "proud" (*huperephanos*) is one who is *unrepentant*. He feels the conviction of the Holy Spirit and knows he's drifted in his devotion to God and needs to come back to Him. But rather than realize how serious his spiritual condition is, he becomes impudent, insolent, and stubborn and won't budge.

Please realize restoration is always God's intention. If one of His children has strayed away from Him, He loves them so much that He will cause His grace to swing into action and set in motion a strategic plan to oppose them and get their attention so they will wake up to their condition, repent, and come back to Him with their whole heart.

God's ultimate goal for every person is summed up beautifully in James 4:10, which says, "Humble yourselves in the sight of the Lord, and he shall lift you up." Clearly, God's desire is to lift us up and restore us in every area of our lives. But before He can do that, He needs us to "humble ourselves." In Greek, this means *to reduce one's self-importance* or *to minimize oneself.* It depicts *one willing to stoop to any measure necessary* in order to get things right with God.

'Speak Not Evil'

As we continue our journey through James 4, keep in mind the people he was writing to were in an all-out verbal war, bickering and judging each other about why certain believers among them were being blessed and others were suffering. James knew the danger of continuing in an atmosphere of criticism and judgment — that it restrains the Holy Spirit from being able to work in people's lives. With this understanding, James said:

> **Speak not evil one of another, brethren. He that speaketh evil of his brother, and judgeth his brother, speaketh evil of the law, and judgeth the law: but if thou judge the law, thou art not a doer of the law, but a judge.**
>
> **— James 4:11**

The phrase "speak not evil" is a translation of the Greek words *me katalaleite.* The word *me* is a negative, thus *a prohibition.* Rather than being a mere suggestion, James was speaking in the strongest and loudest language possible saying, "Stop this! And stop it now! Don't do this anymore." What was he commanding them to stop? The Bible says "speaking evil" — which is the Greek word *katalaleo.* It is a compound of *kata*, meaning *down*, and *laleo*, which means *to talk or to converse.* When compounded, the word *katalaleo* means *to talk down* or *to denigrate.* It denotes *speaking down about someone else* or *to verbally defame a person.*

Therefore, when James said, "Speak not evil...," he was emphatically shouting, "Stop talking down to one another! Stop denigrating and verbally defaming people and stop it now!" Apparently, they were judging one another rather than rejoicing with each other over the blessings of God.

The fact is the flesh always gravitates toward judgment. That's why we must always be on guard not to give into this carnal tendency. When we give place to a mindset of judgment, we begin to speak words of judgment, and what we give to others we will eventually receive from others. That is what was happening among James' readers. They were speaking evil "one of another," which in Greek means *reciprocally, of each other*. Words of judgment and criticism where bouncing back and forth between believers like a tennis ball in a tennis match.

Again, James called the people he was speaking to "brethren," which is a term he used multiple times throughout his letter. It is the Greek word *adelphos*, and it appears three times in this verse alone. It's derived from the word *delphos*, which is the word for *a woman's womb*. When an "a" is attached to the front of the word, it describes *two or more who were born from the same womb*. James used this endearing term again and again to personally connect with his readers. It is as if he was saying, "We're brothers in Christ all born out of the womb of God."

As we've noted, this word was later used in a military sense to denote *brothers in battle, comrades*, or *a brotherhood*. James' use of this term was his way of placing himself side-by-side down in the trenches with his readers. In the context of James 4:11, it is the equivalent of him saying, "Hey brothers, we're all family. We're all fighting the same enemy, and we're fighting together down here in the trenches. We need each other. We're comrades. So please stop talking down to and defaming each other."

Judging Others and Speaking Evil Are One and the Same

James went on to say, "…He that speaketh evil of his brother, and judgeth his brother, speaketh evil of the law, and judgeth the law…" (James 4:11). The word "judgeth" or "judge," which appears four times in this verse, is the Greek word *krino*, a word widely used throughout the New Testament and in secular Greek literature of the First Century. It usually referred to *a jury who had just handed down their final sentence in a court of law* or *a verdict or a final sentence pronounced as the result of a court trial*. After all the evidence had been presented and the judge had examined all the facts, a final verdict was issued by the court. This same word — *krino* — can also be used to describe *one judged by the court of public opinion*.

That's what was going on among these believers James was addressing. Instead of fighting together as comrades in battle against a common enemy, they had turned on each other and were judging one another. The church had become a court of public opinion, and believers were issuing verdicts against other believers without limitation.

To put a stop to this defamation and denigration, James said, "Speak not evil one of another, brethren. He that speaketh evil of his brother, and judgeth his brother, speaketh evil of the law, and judgeth the law..." (James 4:11). This brings us to the word "law," which is the Greek word *nomos*, and refers to the *law of liberty* mentioned in James 1:25. The "law of liberty" is God's Holy Word, and it packs the power to set people free and change lives. This includes the law of Christ, which speaks of loving one another, forgiving one another, and operating in kindness.

Essentially, what James was saying here is, "Brothers, when you talk down to, denigrate, and pronounce judgment on your brothers, you're also issuing a verdict against God's Word and the commandments of Christ — to forgive and love one another. And by doing so, you are not a doer of the law, but a judge."

This phrase "not a doer of the law" in Greek is *ouk ei poietes nomou*. The word *ouk* is *emphatic* and means *absolutely not*. The word *poitetes* describes *a creative doer*, and it is from where we get the word *poet*. Hence, "not a doer of the law" is *one who is absolutely not actively involved in living the Word of God or the commandments of Christ*. Any time we get our eyes off of Jesus and begin using our mouths to criticize and judge others, we fall into this same category of "not a doer of the law."

God Is the One-and-Only Lawgiver Who Has Power To 'Save' and 'Destroy'

Immediately after this, James made this statement: "There is one lawgiver, who is able to save and to destroy: who art thou that judgest another?" (James 4:12) The words "one lawgiver" is a translation of the Greek words *ho vomothetes*, and it means *the one who set the law in place*. The one and only law-giver is God. He and He alone "...is able to save and to destroy..." (James 4:12).

The word "able" here is extraordinary. It is the Greek word *dunamenos* and is derived from the word *dunamai*, which describes *one with power and ability.* Ultimately, the root word of *dunamenos* is the Greek word *dunamis,* which is *explosive, superhuman power that comes with enormous energy and produces phenomenal, extraordinary, and unparalleled results.* It is the same word used by the Roman army to denote the full strength of troops marching forward to take new territory. It was also used by Greeks to depict *a force of nature, like an earthquake, a hurricane, or a tornado.*

Only God — and Jesus His Son — have the immense, supernatural power to "save" someone. This word "save" in Greek is *sodzo,* which means *to heal,* and it also conveys the idea of *wholeness* or *salvation.* Specifically, it denotes *wholeness in every part of life; a touch of salvation that brings delivering and healing power that results in wholeness.*

In addition to having the supernatural power to save, God also has the ability to "destroy." In Greek, the word "destroy" is *apollumi,* and it means *to undo; to destroy;* or *to perish.* Just as only God and Jesus have the power to save a person and produce wholeness in every part of his or her life, they are also the only Ones who have the power to destroy or eternally punish a person.

"Judging people is God's business." That's essentially what James said in verse 12: "…Who art thou that judgest another?" (James 4:12) The phrase "who art thou" in Greek literally says, *"Who, however, are you?"* In modern-day speech, we might say, "Who do you think you are judging another?" This word "another" is *ton plesion,* which includes a definite article and denotes *the one near you, the one living in your neighborhood,* or *the nearby neighbor.*

As we've noted, the believers James was addressing were looking at their fellow comrades in Christ who were literally living right next door and pronouncing all kinds of judgments against each of them. They were doing what only God and His Son Jesus are qualified to do. "Get out of the judgement business," James urged his readers, "and get into the business of fulfilling the law of Christ." Friend, when we give ourselves to the law of Christ, we create a wonderful atmosphere in which the Holy Spirit has full freedom to work!

In our final lesson, we will look at the correct way of talking about and planning for the future and why we need to always include the Holy Spirit.

STUDY QUESTIONS

Study to shew thyself approved unto God, a workman that
needeth not to be ashamed, rightly dividing the word of truth.
— 2 Timothy 2:15

1. According to the original Greek, when we "judge" someone, we're
   issuing a final verdict and passing sentence against them. The danger in
   this is that we can't judge another person fairly or accurately because
   we don't know all the facts and intimate details about their lives. Only
   God is all-knowing and can accurately judge each of us.

   • What does Jesus say about judging others in Matthew 7:1-5 and
     Luke 6:27-38?

   • According to Romans 14:10-13 and First Corinthians 4:5, why is it
     so important that we let go of the gavel and leave the judgment to
     God?

   • Be honest with yourself: Is there anyone you're silently judging —
     or even loudly criticizing — right now at work, in school, church,
     government, or your family? If so, who is it? Why are you frustrated
     with them? In light of this lesson, what do you think you might see
     differently about them?

2. Just before going to the Cross, Jesus gave His disciples — which
   includes us — a new commandment in John 13:34,35, which is sometimes referred to as *the law of Christ.* What is this new commandment
   and how does the apostle Paul reinforce and expand its meaning in
   Ephesians 4:32 and Colossians 3:12,13?

PRACTICAL APPLICATION

But be ye doers of the word, and not hearers only,
deceiving your own selves.
— James 1:22

1. Everything we give to others — including our time, attention, attitudes, resources, and our words — are like seeds we're planting that
   will one day produce a harvest in our own lives. What do Paul's words
   in Galatians 6:7,8 and Jesus' statement in Luke 6:36-38 show you
   about this powerful principle of sowing and reaping?

2. Have you ever had someone speak evil of you? Did they talk down to you or denigrate and defame you to others behind your back? Did they have all the facts right? How did you respond? Knowing the damage words like this can cause, how do you approach the way you talk about others now?

3. Over and over again, God tells us in His Word to get rid of all bitterness and every form of malice and slander (*see* Ephesians 4:29-31; Titus 3:1,2; 1 Peter 2:1). We all know from experience that this is easier said than done. Thankfully, the Holy Spirit is ready, willing, and able to empower you to resist the temptation to speak hate-filled words. Whenever you sense your words are about to take a nosedive, pray something like this:

   "Lord, please help me! I'm really angry and hurting, but I don't want to say hurtful things and become a tool in the enemy's hand. Place a guard over my mouth, heal my heart, and help me only say what will ultimately build others up. Thank You, Lord. In Jesus' name. Amen."

LESSON 5

TOPIC

Planning for Tomorrow and the Future

SCRIPTURES

1. **James 4:13-17** — Go to now, ye that say, To day or to morrow we will go into such a city, and continue there a year, and buy and sell, and get gain: Whereas ye know not what shall be on the morrow. For what is your life? It is even a vapour, that appeareth for a little time, and then vanisheth away. For that ye ought to say, If the Lord will, we shall live, and do this, or that. But now ye rejoice in your boastings: all such rejoicing is evil. Therefore to him that knoweth to do good, and doeth it not, to him it is sin.

GREEK WORDS

1. "go to now" — Ἄγε νῦν (*Age nun*): let me help lead you, now

2. "say" — λέγοντες (*legontes*): refers to an on-going manner of speech; saying and saying

3. "today" — σήμερον (*semeron*): today; this day; right now

4. "tomorrow" — αὔριον (*aurion*): tomorrow; points to the future, particularly tomorrow

5. "go" — πορεύομαι (*poreuomai*): to journey; to move from one place to another; to move to another location for the sake of conducting business

6. "into" — εἰς (*eis*): into; indicating the intention of forward movement

7. "such" — τήνδε (*tende*): emphatically this or that

8. "city" — τὴν πόλιν (*ten polin*): a definite article with πόλις (*polis*); THE city; very clear and specifically-stated plans

9. "continue" — ποιέω (*poieo*): here, to do; to work; to perform; to carry out a pre-planned intention

10. "there" — ἐκεῖ (*ekei*): there; there, in that place; there, in that city

11. "year" — ἐνιαυτός (*eniautos*): a year, or for an exact period of time

12. "buy and sell" — ἐμπορεύομαι (*emporeuomai*): to act as a merchant who buys and sells in a market; to engage in business; to trade in business; where we get the word emporium

13. "get gain" — κερδαίνω (*kerdaino*): to make a gain; to win at a game of business; to play one's cards so well that he wins the game; thus, the intention to win in business and to walk away having made financial gain

14. "whereas ye know not" — οἵτινες οὐκ ἐπίστασθε (*hoitines ouk epistasthe*): οὐκ (*ouk*) is emphatic, and ἐπίσταμαι (*epistamai*) depicts one who is an expert in his knowledge; here, who emphatically does not possess expert insight

15. "what shall be on the morrow" — ‹τὸ› τῆς αὔριον (*to tes aurion*): what will be in the future, even tomorrow

16. "what" — ποία (*poia*): what sort; what kind; what type

17. "your life" — ἡ ζωὴ ὑμῶν (*he zoe humon*): a definite article with ζωή (*zoe*), THE life of yours; the life you possess

18. "for" — γάρ ἐστε (*gar este*): a conjunction; for isn't it; for it is

19. "vapour" — ἀτμίς (*atmis*): used by Aristotle, Herodotus, and Plato to describe a vapor, steam, or a mist

20. "appeareth" — **φαινομένη** (*phainomene*): from **φαίνω** (*phaino*) meaning to appear, to become visible; to shine

21. "for a little time" — **πρὸς ὀλίγον** (*pros oligon*): the word **ὀλίγος** (*oligos*) means small in number; here it refers to a small amount of time of a small number of years; something that is brief; for a short duration of time; for a short period of time; for a little time

22. "then" — **ἔπειτα** (*epeita*): thereafter; after that; indicates something that occurs suddenly

23. "vanisheth away" — **ἀφανίζω** (*aphanidzo*): it quickly passes from the scene, disappearing and becoming invisible

24. "for that ye ought" — **ἀντὶ** (*anti*): instead

25. "to say" — **λέγειν** (*legein*): to say

26. "if" — **ἐάν** (*ean*): the idea of a certain possibility; in all likelihood, it probably will happen

27. "Lord" — **Κύριος** (*Kurios*): Lord; Supreme Master; the One to Whom we defer and obey

28. "will" — **θέλω** (*thelo*): future tense of **θέλω** (*thelo*), to intend, to design, to desire

29. "shall live" — **ζήσομεν** (*zesomen*): plural, we will live

30. "we will do" — **ποιήσομεν** (*poiesomen*): plural, we will carry on, we will be productive

31. "this or that" — **τοῦτο ἢ ἐκεῖνο** (*touto e ekeino*): this or that; this here, or that yonder

32. "but now" — **νῦν δὲ** (*nun de*): now, however; now, instead

33. "rejoice" — **καυχάομαι** (*kauchaomai*): projects the image of a head held high; an arrogant attitude

34. "boastings" — **ἀλαζονεία** (*aladzoneia*): the word used to depict frauds who roamed from place to place and who possessed "cures" to rid people of all their ills; empty promises; insolent and arrogant claims

35. "all" — **πᾶσα** (*pasa*): all; an all-inclusive term

36. "such" — **τοιοῦτος** (*toioutos*): such; such a thing; pointing to something specific

37. "rejoicing" — **καυχάομαι** (*kauchaomai*): projects the image of a head held high; an arrogant attitude

38. "evil" — **πονηρός** (*poneros*): destruction, disaster, harm, or danger; malicious or malignant; foul, vile, hostile, and vicious; it includes not

only that which is dangerous to the physical body but also to that which is dangerous to the spirit or mind; it is often used in the Greek Septuagint version of the Old Testament to describe actions that are damaging to a person's testimony and reputation; can depict actions, laws, or people, whose behavior is opposed to the righteous nature of God

39. "therefore" — οὖν (*oun*): therefore; consequently; hence; as a result

40. "to him that knoweth" — εἰδότι (*eidoti*): from οἶδα, meaning to comprehend; for the one who really knows and comprehends

41. "to do good" — καλὸν ποιεῖν (*kalon poiein*): from καλός (*kalos*) and ποιέω (*poieo*) the word καλός (*kalos*) pictures something that is fitting, noble, or admirable; the word ποιέω (*poieo*) means to do; here, to do that which is fitting, right, and noble

42. "doeth it not" — μὴ ποιοῦντι (*me poiounti*): and is not doing it

43. "to him" — αὐτῷ (*auto*): to him; especially to him

44. "sin" — ἁμαρτία (*hamartia*): sin; falling short of what is right and expected by God; totally missing the mark

SYNOPSIS

As we have noted throughout this study, the book of James was written by the half-brother of Jesus, and he wrote to the Jewish believers from the 12 tribes of Jacob who had been scattered abroad by the persecution of the Roman Empire (*see* James 1:1). These First-Century Christians had lost their homes, their jobs, their friends, and their family connections. Consequently, they were really struggling to hang on to their faith and trust in God.

It appears from James' writing in chapter 4 that many of these believers were doing everything in their power to regain what they had lost and reestablish themselves in business. The problem was, they were operating in their own fleshly strength, and they hadn't prayed and asked for God's input or help. And even the ones who did pray did so with selfish motives.

Making matters worse, an atrocious war of words broke out, where those who were being blessed by God were being viciously judged and defamed by those who were still waiting for a breakthrough. Before long, the law of sowing and reaping kicked in, causing judgment to give way to more judgment. This low-level carnality soon began to spread and affect the minds of believers with regard to how they were planning for the future, which is what we're focusing on in this lesson.

The emphasis of this lesson:

Making detailed plans without God's involvement is always a bad idea. We have no clue about what tomorrow holds. Our life is like a fleeting vapor or blip on the screen of time that's here today and quickly disappears. Rather than arrogantly boast and brag about what we intend to do, we should have a humble, God-honoring attitude regarding all future plans.

Although there's nothing wrong with making plans about what you would like to do in the days ahead, none of us should make plans without seeking the Lord's direction in prayer. Unfortunately, many believers make plans independent of God, which is what it appears the believers James was writing to were doing. He said:

> **Go to now, ye that say, To day or to morrow we will go into such a city, and continue there a year, and buy and sell, and get gain: Whereas ye know not what shall be on the morrow. For what is your life? It is even a vapour, that appeareth for a little time, and then vanisheth away. For that ye ought to say, If the Lord will, we shall live, and do this, or that. But now ye rejoice in your boastings: all such rejoicing is evil. Therefore to him that knoweth to do good, and doeth it not, to him it is sin.**
> **— James 4:13-17**

To make sure we receive all that the Holy Spirit is speaking through James in this passage, let's take the remainder of this lesson and unpack the original Greek meanings of the key words in each verse.

Making Detailed Plans Without God's Involvement Is a Bad Idea
James 4:13

Looking again at James 4:13, it says:

> **Go to now, ye that say, To day or to morrow we will go into such a city, and continue there a year, and buy and sell, and get gain.**

The phrase "go to now" in Greek is *Age nun*, a compound of the words *Age* and *nun*. The word *Age* means *I lead*, and the word *nun* means *right now*. When these words come together to form *Age nun*, it indicates James is literally saying, "Let me help lead you, right now...."

From here he begins to give specific guidance to people who "say" what they're going to do. This word "say" is the Greek word *legontes*, which means *alleging*. The tense here refers to *an on-going manner of speech*, which means it could be translated "You who are *saying and saying and saying*," or "You who *keep alleging* and *keep claiming*..."

What did they keep saying? "Today or tomorrow we will go into such a city...." The word "today" in Greek is *semeron*, which means *today; this day; or right now*. The word "tomorrow" is the Greek word *aurion*, and it means *tomorrow*. It points to the future, particularly *tomorrow*. These individuals were saying and saying where they were planning to "go."

In Greek, the word "go" is *poreuomai*, and it means *to journey* or *to move from one place to another*. It can also indicate *moving to another location for the sake of conducting business*. Keep in mind these are Jews who have made the decision to trust Jesus as their Messiah, Lord, and Savior. They had lost virtually everything as a result of Roman persecution, and now they were trying to reestablish their homes and livelihood.

They said, "Today or tomorrow we will go into such a city...." The word "into" here is a form of the Greek word *eis*, which means *into* and indicates *the intention of forward movement*. The word "such" means *emphatically this or that*, and the word "city" in Greek is *ten polin*, which has a definite article with *polis*, meaning *THE city*. In other words, these were *very clear and specifically stated plans*.

Not only were these believers making very specific plans, but they also said, "...[We will] continue there a year, and buy and sell, and get gain" (James 4:13). The word "continue" is actually a poor translation. It is the Greek word *poieo*, which here means *to do; to work; to perform; to carry out a pre-planned intention*. The word "there" in Greek is *ekei*, meaning *there, in that particular place; there, in that city*.

The word "year" means *a year* or *for an exact period of time*. These believers claimed they were going to stay in a specific place for an exact period of time in order to "buy and sell." In Greek, "buy and sell" is the word *emporeuomai*, which is where we get the word *emporium*, the word for *a very large marketplace.* This word *emporeuomai* means *to act as a merchant who buys and sells in a market; to engage in business;* or *to trade in business.*

Basically, these Jewish believers were saying over and over again that they were about to make a great deal of money by engaging in business — buying and selling goods — in a particular city for a particular length of time. Their goal was to "get gain," which is a translation of the Greek word *kerdaino,* meaning *to make a gain* or *to win at the game of business.* It carries the idea of playing one's cards so well that he wins the game. Thus, the intention here is to win in business and walk away having made financial gain.

Taking into account the original Greek meaning of these words, here is the *Renner Interpretive Version (RIV)* of James 4:13

> **Let me provide some guidance for you who are constantly saying, 'Right now, today, tomorrow, or in the nearest future, we are going on a business trip and will travel into a particular city with the intention to stay there to do a lot of buying, selling, and business. Our intention is to walk away with a big financial profit.**

We Are Clueless About What Tomorrow Holds
James 4:14

After James recited to his readers the kinds of things they were saying about their future plans, he began to paint a picture of just how fleeting life is. He said:

> **Whereas ye know not what shall be on the morrow. For what is your life? It is even a vapour, that appeareth for a little time, and then vanisheth away.**
> > **—James 4:14**

The phrase "whereas ye know not" in Greek is *hoitines ouk epistasthe.* The word *ouk* here is an emphatic *no,* and the word *epistamai* (the root of *epistasthe*) depicts *one who is an expert in his knowledge.* In context here, the collective meaning of this phrase is *one who emphatically does not possess expert insight.* James was basically saying, "You don't have a clue 'what shall be on the morrow,'" or "You don't have the foggiest idea of what will be in the future, even tomorrow."

He then rhetorically asked, "…For what is your life?" (James 4:14) The word "what" here is the Greek word *poia*, meaning *what sort*, *what kind*, or *what type*. "Your life" in Greek is *he zoe humon*, which includes a definite article and literally means *THE life of yours* or *THE life you possess*.

In this verse, James answers his own question saying, "…It is even a vapour…" (James 4:14). In Greek, this word "vapour" is *atmis*, and it describes *a vapor*, *steam*, or *a mist*. It was used by Aristotle, Herodotus, and Plato in their writings. In the big scheme of things, our human life is a blip on the screen of time.

Like the steam rising from a pot of boiling water or a vapor of smoke from a fresh fire, "…[Your life] appeareth for a little time, and then vanisheth away" (James 4:14). The word "appeareth" is the Greek word *phainomene*, from *phaino*, which means *to appear*, *to become visible*, or *to shine*. Indeed, some people's lives really shine, but their glimmer is short-lived.

That is why James said it appears "for a little time." This phrase is a translation of the Greek words *pros oligon*. The word *oligos* means *small in number*, and here it refers to *a small amount of time* or *a small number of years*. It denotes *something that is brief*, *something that exists for a short duration of time* or *for a short period of time*.

James said we are here for a short duration of time, "…then vanisheth away" (James 4:14). The word "then" is the Greek word *epeita*, which means *thereafter* or *after that* and indicates *something that occurs suddenly*. One minute it's here, and then "Poof!" — it's gone. The phrase "vanisheth away" is a translation of the Greek word *aphanidzo*, meaning *it quickly passes from the scene, disappearing and becoming invisible*.

Taking into account the original Greek meaning of these words, here is the *Renner Interpretive Version (RIV)* of James 4:14:

> **But… hold on… what sort of life is yours anyway? Isn't it like a vapor or mist that suddenly becomes visible and only shines for a relatively brief time? And then — poof, it suddenly evaporates, passes from the scene, and it's gone.**

Have a 'God-Willing' Approach To Planning
James 4:15

In verse 15, James offered his readers a more accurate, God-honoring way of making plans for tomorrow and the future. He said:

> **For that ye ought to say, If the Lord will, we shall live, and do this, or that.**
> — James 4:15

When James said, "For that ye ought," it is a translation of the Greek word *anti*, which would better be translated as, "Instead, what you ought...." The words "to say" in Greek is *legein*, and it indicates *instruction concerning what one should say regarding the future.*

"If the Lord will" is also an important phrase. The word "if" is the Greek word *ean*, and it expresses *the idea of a certain possibility*. It is the equivalent of saying, *"In all likelihood, it probably will happen."* The word "Lord" in Greek is *Kurios*, which means *Lord* or *Supreme Master; the One to Whom we defer and obey*. This refers to Jesus, and the very fact that He is *Supreme Master* means He has the right to change our plans at any moment.

It is the Lord's *will* that we want. The Greek word for "will" here is the future tense of the word *thelo*, and it means *to intend, to design*, or *to desire*. Hence, we want to walk out and experienced what *the Lord intends and has designed for our lives*. He knows what is truly best.

James says that when it comes to planning for the future, we should say, "...If the Lord will, we shall live, and do this, or that" (James 4:15). In Greek, the latter part of this verse is translated, "We will live and we will carry on, we will be productive in this or that; this here or that yonder."

Taking into account the original Greek meaning of these words, here is the *Renner Interpretive Version (RIV)* of James 4:15:

> **Instead of so brashly proclaiming what you are going to do, it would be better to say, 'If the Lord plans, designs, and desires it — and in all likelihood, it seems that is the case — then we have the intention of being here or there, and doing this or that.**

Don't Brag About What You Don't Know

James 4:16

In verse 16, James reverted back to correction mode, pointing out the error in the way his readers were speaking. He said:

> **But now ye rejoice in your boastings: all such rejoicing is evil.**
> — James 4:16

The opening words "but now" are the Greek words *nun de*. A more literal translation of this phrase would be *now, however* or *now, instead*. Hence, James said, "Now, however, ye rejoice…," or "Now, instead, ye rejoice…." In Greek, the word "rejoice" is *kauchaomai*, and it projects *the image of a head held high*. It is *an arrogant attitude of a person brazenly making a proclamation*.

This brings us to the word "boastings," which is the Greek word *aladzoneia*, the word used to depict *frauds who roamed from place to place and who possessed "cures" to rid people of all their ills*. Thus, this word "boastings" could be translated as *empty promises* or *insolent and arrogant claims*.

James said, "…All such rejoicing is evil" (James 4:16). The word "all" is the Greek word *pasa*, which means *all* and is an all-inclusive term — *absolutely all* such rejoicing. The word "such" in Greek is *toioutos*, meaning *such a thing* and *points to something specific*.

The word "rejoicing" is again the Greek word *kauchaomai*, which depicts *an arrogant attitude of a person brazenly making boasts and claims without praying and consulting the Lord*. James says absolutely all of these braggadocious assertions are "evil."

In Greek, the word "evil" is *poneros*, a word synonymous with *destruction, disaster, harm*, or *danger*. It describes *something malicious or malignant*; *something foul, vile, hostile*, and *vicious*. It includes not only that which is dangerous to the physical body but also that which is dangerous to the spirit or mind. It is often used in the Greek Septuagint version of the Old Testament to describe *actions that are damaging to a person's testimony and reputation*. It can also depict actions, laws, or people whose behavior is opposed to the righteous nature of God.

Taking into account the original Greek meaning of these words, here is the *Renner Interpretive Version (RIV)* of James 4:16:

However, right now you are arrogantly boasting and bragging about what you are planning to do. Your talk reminds me of those well-known roaming shysters who purport to know everything but can't deliver on the empty promises they make. All boasting of this type is destructive, dangerous, and harmful, and furthermore, if you make a bunch of claims that you can't deliver on, it will ruin your testimony with those who heard you boasting and bragging.

When You Know Better, Do Better
James 4:17

James concluded his discussion on planning for tomorrow and the future with this sobering warning:

> **Therefore to him that knoweth to do good, and doeth it not, to him it is sin.**
> — **James 4:17**

The word "therefore" is the Greek word *oun*, and it means *therefore* or *consequently*. Hence, it could be translated *as a result*. The phrase "to him that knoweth" is a translation of the Greek word *eidoti*, which is from *oida*, meaning *to comprehend* or *for the one who really knows and comprehends*.

James said, "To this very one who really knows and comprehends...." Then he adds the phrase "to do good," which in Greek is *kalon poiein* and is derived from the words *kalos* and *poieo*. The word *kalos* pictures *something that is fitting, noble, or admirable*; and the word *poieo* means *to do*. When these two words are compounded, it means *to do that which is fitting, right, and noble*.

Anyone who really knows and comprehends doing what is fitting, right, and noble and "...doeth it not, to him it is sin" (James 4:17). The words "doeth it not" — the Greek words *me poiounti* — mean *and is not doing it*. The phrase "to him" in Greek is a translation of the word *auto*, meaning *to him* or *especially to him*. And the word "sin" is the Greek word *hamartia*, which describes *sin* or *falling short of what is right and expected by God*. It is *the picture of one totally missing the mark*.

Taking into account the original Greek meaning of these words, here is the *Renner Interpretive Version (RIV)* of James 4:17:

> **Therefore, for the one who really gets the message of what I'm saying — I'm talking about the one who gets it so well that he knows what is the right thing to do — but he nevertheless fails to do it — that person's failure to do what is right is a sin. Make no mistake, that person is totally missing the mark and falling short of what is right and expected by God.**

Friend, if there was ever a time that we needed God's involvement for our plans for tomorrow and the future, it is now. He alone is all-knowing and can direct us with supernatural precision. His gift to us is His amazing Holy Spirit, and Jesus said the Spirit "…shall guide you into all truth, for he will not be presenting his own ideas, but will be passing on to you what he has heard. He will tell you about the future" (John 16:13 *TLB*).

Friend, begin investing in your relationship with the Holy Spirit. Seek His face daily by reading the Word and opening your heart to Him in prayer. As you do, you will taste and see that the Lord is good, and that the partnership of His Spirit is truly priceless!

STUDY QUESTIONS

> Study to shew thyself approved unto God, a workman that
> needeth not to be ashamed, rightly dividing the word of truth.
> — 2 Timothy 2:15

1. The word "rejoice" in Greek depicts *the image of a head held high*. It is *an arrogant attitude of a person brazenly making a proclamation*. Countless people throughout history have acted this way — including these three individuals listed below. According to Scripture, how was their arrogance displayed? What ended up happening? What do these examples speak to you personally?
   - **Rich man** (*see* Luke 12:15-21)
   - **Herod** (*see* Acts 12:20-23)
   - **Nebuchadnezzar** (*see* Daniel 4:28-37)

2. Remember what we learned in Lesson 3 about pride? When we have a prideful, boasting attitude about where we're going and what we're doing, God will oppose us. But what happens when we acknowledge Him and commit our plans to Him? (*See* Proverbs 3:5-8; 16:1-3,9; and also consider Psalm 32:8; Isaiah 30:21; and John 16:13.)

3. Do you think that Jesus had hyper-defined plans for His ministry? According to Mark 1:35, what was the secret of the effectiveness of His ministry? (Also consider the prophecy about Him in Isaiah 50:4,5.)

PRACTICAL APPLICATION

But be ye doers of the word, and not hearers only,
deceiving your own selves.
—James 1:22

1. When was the last time someone made an empty promise to you? How did you feel when you realized they weren't going to follow through? What did the experience teach you about the value of being careful with your own words and promises for the future?

2. Have you ever made an extremely well-thought-out plan — a plan you were proud of, and thought was foolproof — only for it to fall apart when something unexpected happened? How did that experience shape your thinking about making future plans? Did it make you more or less likely to put your trust in your own ability to plan?

3. Trusting in God day by day and for the future is the smartest decision you can make as you move forward from this teaching. Get alone with the Lord and take time to meditate on the priceless wisdom found in Proverbs 3:5-8. Let these timeless words become engraved on your heart and mind as you surrender the leadership of your life afresh to Him.

Notes

_____

_____

_____

_____

_____

_____

_____

_____

_____

_____

_____

_____

_____

_____

_____

_____

_____

_____

_____

_____

_____

_____

_____

_____

_____

_____

_____

_____

Notes

www.ingramcontent.com/pod-product-compliance
Lightning Source LLC
Chambersburg PA
CBHW051047030426
42339CB00006B/231